James Mavor

The English Railway Rate Question

James Mavor

The English Railway Rate Question

ISBN/EAN: 9783744725576

Printed in Europe, USA, Canada, Australia, Japan

Cover: Foto ©ninafisch / pixelio.de

More available books at **www.hansebooks.com**

THE ENGLISH RAILWAY RATE QUESTION.

BY

JAMES MAVOR.

Reprinted from the (Harvard) " Quarterly Journal of Economics,"
Vol. viii., No. 3; April, 1894

THE ENGLISH RAILWAY RATE QUESTION.

I.

THE chief stages in English railway history may be described as follows: —

First. There was the period of doubt and suspicion as regards the national advantage and probable financial success of railways. This period was short. It really extended only from the promotion of the Liverpool and Manchester Railway in 1824 until about 1840. Even while it endured there were incipient movements towards governmental encouragement of railway enterprise; for Parliament was induced to grant a loan to the Liverpool Railway of $500,000, at 3½ per cent. interest,—a low rate at the time. Parliament also exempted it from the passenger tax which was then payable by stage-coaches. This tax was practically imposed upon the railways in 1832; but the terms of its imposition gave the railways an advantage over stage-coaches which amounted to a not inconsiderable bounty.*

Second. The great change in the attitude of Parliament and the public towards railways came about in the *second* period, when "the extreme of determined rejection or dilatory acquiescence" was exchanged for "the opposite extreme of unlimited concession." † This, however, is putting the case rather too strongly. The concessions were never unlimited, although they were large. Even at that time the powers of the railway companies were defined by act of Parliament. The promoters of the companies were shrewd enough to ask not for vague powers,

* *Cf.* Thomas Grahame, *Treatise on Inland Intercourse in Civilized States*, 1834, p. 106 *et seq.*

† Quoted by Herbert Spencer, "Railway Morals and Railways Policy," *Essays*, American edition, p. 265.

— for vagueness is a two-edged weapon in a statute,— but for large, definite powers. For example, the maximum rates for which they asked were largely in excess of what they intended to charge, and largely in excess also of what they did charge until the inflation of trade in 1870–74. They left a large margin for contingencies, but they demanded definite powers. Railway enterprise was encouraged by these statutory privileges; and the increase of railway dividends, due to the rapid expansion of traffic and the relatively high rates, produced the railway mania of 1845. The railway Acts passed during this period were formed upon a definite model, and in one of the clauses of this model Act the principles of equal mileage and of equal treatment were laid down.*

The Regulation of Railways Act of 1844† gave powers to the Treasury to revise the scale of "tolls, fares, and charges" of any railway company, when the dividends of the company exceeded 10 per cent.‡ The Railway Clauses Act of 1845 § enabled the railway companies to

---

* "The rates and tolls to be taken by virtue of this Act shall at all times be charged equally, and after the same rate per ton per mile throughout the whole of the said railway in respect of the same description of articles, matters, or things, and that no reduction or advance in the said rates and tolls shall, directly or indirectly, be made partially or in favor of or against any particular person or company, or be confined to any particular part of said railway, but that every such reduction or advance of rates and tolls upon any particular kind or description of articles . . . shall extend to and take place throughout the whole and every part of said railway . . . and shall extend to all persons . . . using the same."

See copy in Grierson, *Railway Rates, English and Foreign*, 1886, Appendix, p. lxxi.

† 7 & 8 *Vict.*, c. 85.

‡ This limitation has been rather scornfully treated by critics of English railway policy, and no doubt with some justice, when regarded from the point of view of more recent practices of stock-watering, etc., which must render ineffectual dividend limitations pure and simple. In 1845, however, the railway system was yet in its raw youth; and the anxiety of the legislature led it to the adoption of any feasible plan of preventing the railway companies from assuming the position of monopolies. The limitation must be judged in the light of experience at the time when it was enacted. The force and interest of it, apart from questions of the easiness of evasion, vary with the dividends.

§ 8 & 9 *Vict.*, c. 20.

vary the tolls upon the railway "so as to accommodate them to the circumstances of the traffic," thus withdrawing the "equal mileage" clauses of the earlier Acts. The same Act re-enacted the prohibition of "prejudicing or favoring particular parties."

During the period from about 1840 until 1854 the railway network of England was practically created. It is true that this network was built on no definite plan, that it was financed on no very sound principles, that there was much chicanery in promotion, and much mismanagement afterwards. Yet it was made, and made quickly,—made much more quickly, perhaps, than it could have been made, had any other system been adopted. But the want of a plan, besides causing great waste of resources, resulted in discontinuity of lines. Transference of traffic from one line to another was inconveniently conducted, and sometimes even wilfully impeded. Combination or amalgamation of lines became both a public necessity and a public danger. Parliament endeavored to control amalgamations by still more strenuously defining the powers of the companies. But the administration of such laws is always hard; and the mere repetition in successive Acts of clauses against undue preference, etc., suggests that the clauses in the earlier Acts had been disregarded.

Third. In order to obviate the inconveniences referred to, the Railway Traffic Act of 1854 * "was passed, with the object of securing facilities for through or other traffic" and "equal treatment for all persons and articles." † This act probably marks the beginning of effective control, and may thus be held to indicate the beginning of the *third* period. During this period, extending perhaps from 1854 to about 1870, there was in England a struggle in railway policy, as indeed in general industrial policy, between a tendency towards diminution of State

---

* 17 & 18 *Vict.*, c. 31.

† See *Fourteenth Report Railway Commissioners*, 1888, p. 3.

control over industry and commerce, and a tendency towards increase of this control. And there can be no doubt that the latter tendency won, at all events, for the time.

Fourth. This victory marks the beginning of the *fourth* period. Until about 1870 the presumption was against State and municipal control of any public service which was thought capable of being performed by private enterprise. From that date the presumption has been quite the contrary.*

In conformity with the tendency of the time the Railway Regulation Act of 1868 † developed the system of control. The greatly increased traffic had brought into existence conditions which could not have been foreseen, and therefore could not have been made the subject of legislation in earlier Acts. Among the new provisions in the Act of 1868 was one upon a subject of which more will be heard later; namely, specification of charge. Under Section 17 of that Act the railway companies were bound to furnish particulars of the charges for goods, and to differentiate between "conveyance of goods on the railway, including therein tolls for the use of the railway, for the use of carriages, and for locomotive power," and so much of the charge as may be "for loading and unloading, covering, collection, and delivery." The next important stage in the fourth period is marked by the Report of the Committee of 1872, and the consequent legislation of 1873. The economical conditions of the time must be kept carefully in view in examining the conclusions of this Report as well as in weighing the evidence given before the committee. For two years trade had been advancing "by leaps and bounds." The traffic receipts of the rail-

*The purchase of the telegraphs by the government, 1867-68; the General Tramways Act of 1870, which gave large powers to municipalities; the numerous gas and water bills promoted by municipalities,—are a few among the many manifestations of this tendency about 1870.

† 31 & 32 *Vict.*, c. 119.

way companies increased 20 per cent. between 1869 and 1872. The proportion of net receipts to capital advanced from 3.91 per cent. in 1867 and 4.22 per cent. in 1869 to 4.74 per cent. in 1872,—a point which they have never since reached. Rates had gone up considerably. The railway companies were doing their utmost to reap a full share of the golden harvest, and the possibilities of their reaping an inordinate share did not appear remote. Thus there naturally arose demands for legislative interference to prevent the railways from taking an excessive advantage of the powers over inland transport which amalgamation had secured to them.

In the discussions before the legislation of 1873 it was the interest of both parties in the controversy to minimize the effect of previous legislation. The traders adopted this attitude because they wanted new and more stringent acts, and they had to show that the existing acts were inadequate; and the railway companies had to show that all legislation of a restrictive kind was useless and pernicious. These dialectical expedients, to which the commissioners of 1872 fell easy victims, ought not, however, to betray us into the belief that the legislation up to 1873 was wholly futile. It is difficult to believe that the railway system would have or could have safely developed with greater rapidity; and it would be difficult to prove that any other policy could wisely have been adopted than that which retained the general principle in all Acts, that a railway company was wholly a creature of statute, and that special conditions should be legislated for as they emerged.

From 1854 until 1872 the railway companies were obviously not allowed to do as they pleased, but they were given extensive powers. To call this system *laissez-faire* is to misapply the expression.* It is rather a sys-

* *Cf.* Adams, *Railroads, their Origin and Problems*, p. 94, for a contrary opinion.

tem of limited ownership and controlled administration. The English railway policy has been of this nature from the beginning; as we shall see from its more recent history, it has been, for good or evil, a policy of progressive intensification of control. Whether the policy is justifiable or not on abstract grounds, the railway companies have never been free from the leash of the State, and are now more constrained by it than ever. Nor has the policy as disclosed by the statutes been wholly ineffective.

The impetuous conclusion of the Committee of 1872, to the effect that English legislation had never accomplished anything which it sought to bring about or prevented anything which it sought to hinder, is a piece of rhetorical exaggeration which is responsible for much misunderstanding of the English system. The same phrase is applied by Mr. Herbert Spencer to all legislation, and is perhaps in some measure true as a general statement; but it has no peculiar application to railway law. The committee were judging the existing legislation in the light of the situation in 1872, and were not taking into account the general history of English railway policy. No doubt each step had been looked upon, when it was made, as the final one. But this error is not peculiar to railway history, and it is not matter of surprise that the rapid growth of the railway system should have brought frequent need for amendments to the original legislation.

The main point in the discussions of 1872–73 was the question of "undue preference." This was an old question: it had been dealt with in every Act, yet it appeared in full vigor before the Committee of 1872. The reason is not far to seek. Railway rates had been comparatively stationary for some years, until the expansion of trade brought a movement of general rates upwards. Even if the railway companies had not entertained the sinister design of taking a high rate wherever they could get it, and of disregarding the explicit prohibition in these

Acts of Parliament, there would still have been room for the existence of "undue preferences," and for grumbling about them whether they existed or not. It is small wonder, therefore, that the cry of "undue preferences" should have been the leading one at this period. Perhaps the suggestion implies too great astuteness on the part of the railway managers; but it may be that they saw the advantage of accepting as the issue of the inevitable battle between the railways and the public, so comparatively trivial an issue as "undue preference." Whether or not this was their intention, it is clear that the selection of this issue for the fight of 1872-73 led to the postponement for nearly twenty years of the much more serious discussion in regard to the regulation of railway rates. The principal outcome of the legislation of 1873 was the establishment of a new tribunal to try railway causes. The Railway Commissioners' Court was avowedly an experiment.* It has probably, on the whole, fulfilled its function. Appeal to it is not much less expensive to litigants than appeal to the ordinary law courts, but its existence has no doubt exercised an important check upon the giving of "undue preferences." In recent discussions on railway management the question of individual discriminations has dropped out of the field.†

The settlement effected by the Act of 1873 was not disturbed until about 1880, when the question of differential rates,— or of unequal mileage rates,— of low rates for long-distance traffic and relatively high rates for short-distance traffic (the short-haul question), emerged in cases before the Commissioners and also before the law courts.‡

---

* Professor Hadley's criticism (*Railroad Transportation*, p. 177) seems to me quite just. The Railway Commission is neither a conspicuous success nor a conspicuous failure.

† A useful summary of important decisions is given by Professor Hadley, *Railroad Transportation*, p. 183.

‡ Especially *Budd* v. *London & North-Western Railway*, 36 L. T., N. S., p. 802, and *Denaby Colliery Co.* v. *Manchester, Sheffield & Lincoln Railway*, *Seventh Report Railway Commissioners*, p. 5.

According to decisions in these cases, differential rates were illegal; and the result was an agitation mainly in the interests of the traders whose traffic was purely local. The Select Committee of 1881–82 was therefore appointed to deal with this aspect of the question of discriminatory rates. From the first it was evident that this committee would arrive at nothing. It was too large and heterogeneous for serious inquiry into a highly complicated problem. The committee defended differential rates against the adverse judgment of the law courts, but recommended no legislation,—a futile proceeding, which left the rates question in a worse muddle than ever. This was soon made evident in the renewed agitation which took place almost immediately after the report was issued.

Fifth. This agitation did not devote itself to the abstract question of discriminatory rates, but was directed towards an all-round reduction of rates. " The subject of *differential* rates became really a subordinate one. It was the question of *exorbitant* rates that most agitated the public mind." * The agitation and its results cover the *fifth* stage of English railway history.

The beginning of the period extending from 1873 until 1878–79 was a period of high prosperity : the end was a period of depression. In 1880–81 there was again a revival; in 1882 trade was brisk ; but in 1883–84 began the period known as the Great Depression, which reached its lowest point in 1886. These occurrences have been recited because it is impossible to dissociate attacks upon the railways by the public from the general economic movement. The inflation of trade had led to increase of rates, and now the depression of trade led to demands that they should be decreased. Clamor for reduction of railway rates was coincident with the fall of prices. But, in order to meet the expanding traffic during the period of

* An inversion of a statement by Professor Hadley regarding the previous period. The whole situation had altered by the time Professor Hadley's book was in the press. Cf. *Railroad Transportation*, p. 180.

inflation, the railway companies had expended great sums
in extensions, and especially in stations in the large centres of population. Much of this additional capital was as
yet unremunerative or not fully remunerative. The proportion of net receipts to total paid up capital fell from
4.74 per cent. in 1872 to 4.15 per cent. in 1879. It rose to
4.29 per cent. in 1883, and fell to 4.16 per cent. in 1884,
to 4.02 per cent. in 1885, and to 3.99 per cent. in 1886.
The traders were feeling the pinch of the times, and, in
face of a diminishing volume of business and diminishing
amount of profits, were anxious to obtain reduction in railway rates; while for the same reasons the railway companies were anxious to keep them up. In 1884 the railway
companies embarked in a policy which, from a tactical
point of view, was very questionable, and was necessarily
unsuccessful. Their rates in many cases already approached the maximum rates, and they knew that it was
futile to attempt to induce Parliament to increase these
maximum rates; but they determined to make use of the
argument that they had expended large sums upon terminal facilities, in order to obtain legislative sanction for
charging separately for these terminals. The policy was
inexpedient, because it raised a question which it was not
for the interest of the railway companies to raise; and it
was defeated because of the overwhelming opposition of
the traders. Moreover, the battle was a useless one. It
need never have been fought. The railway companies
had the power to charge for terminals, and had been
habitually charging for them. It is true, this proceeding
was called in question; but in 1885 the decision in the
case of *Hall* v. *The London, Brighton & South Coast
Railway,** in the special case brought before the Court of
the Queen's Bench on the instructions of the Railway
Commissioners, settled the law of the question in favor
of the railway companies. It was held that they had un-

---

* *Law Reports, Queen's Bench Division*, vol. xv. p. 505.

limited powers to charge "a reasonable sum," and for the determination of what constituted a reasonable sum there was nothing but the common-law machinery. In asking for definite powers, it is clear that they made a mistake.

The Report of the Royal Commission on Depression of Trade affords a considerable amount of evidence upon the views of the traders in regard to railway rates during the depression. There can be no doubt that the traders were irritated by the fall in prices and the absence of a corresponding reduction in the cost of transport.*

The shelving of the problem by the Committee of 1881–82, the failure of the railway companies to carry their proposals through Parliament, and the increasing complexity of the rates system, due to the development of differential tariffs, had brought the railway system into a condition of chaos. No doubt the traders exaggerated the difficulties of the situation, but it is certain that it had become too highly complex for the conservative and indolent mind of the English trader. He did not know what he was to be charged for the goods he despatched, and he objected to terminals which he did not understand and to which he affected to be unaccustomed.

The mere evolution of industry contributed to this confusion. The Clearing-House Classification had grown by accretion until it reached 4,000 items: the rates had multiplied until they became hundreds of millions. Some simplification appeared advisable, and the Government was ultimately induced to undertake it. Besides, it seemed that action of some kind was necessary to relieve the pressure upon the miscellaneous trades,† which were suffering from the depression and were powerful enough to make their clamor heeded; while, on the other hand, railway interests were no longer so formidable in Parlia-

* See below, p. 294.

† On the development of the miscellaneous trades at this time, see Mr. Giffen's Address to Section F, British Association, 1887.

ment as once they were.* Therefore, the government
(Lord Salisbury's) brought in and carried the Railway
and Canal Traffic Act of 1888.† This Act practically
intrusted the Board of Trade with the formulation of
a thorough-going revision alike of classification and of
rates.‡ It also reorganized the Railway Commission,§ en-
dowed the Board of Trade with the privileges of a "can-
did friend" of the railways and of the traders alike,
entitling it to receive complaints from traders, and to
confer with the railway managers on the subject of these
complaints, without, however, giving the Board any magis-
terial powers regarding either the railways or the traders
in these matters. ‖ These complaints were to be made
the subject of annual reports to Parliament. The railway companies were also required to render to the Board
of Trade such statements as the Board might from time
to time prescribe.¶

In undertaking the revision of the classification and the
maximum rates, the following procedure was prescribed:
Every railway company was required to submit to the
Board of Trade "a revised classification of merchandise
traffic, and a revised schedule of maximum rates and
charges applicable thereto, proposed to be charged," and
to state fully "the nature and amounts of all terminal
charges proposed to be authorized in respect of each class
of traffic, and the circumstances under which such terminal charges are proposed to be made. In the determination of the terminal charges of any railway company
regard shall be had only to the expenditure reasonably
necessary to provide the accommodation in respect of
which such charges are made, irrespective of the outlay
which may have been actually incurred by the railway
company in providing that accommodation." **

* *Financial Reform Almanac*, 1891, p. 129.   † 51 & 52 *Vict.*, c. 25.

‡ *Ibid.*, Part II., §§ 24–30.   § *Ibid.*, Part I., §§ 2–23.   ‖ *Ibid.*, § 31.

¶ *Ibid.*, § 32.   ** *Ibid.*, § 24, subsection 1.

The classification and schedule were to be submitted within six months,—extensions of time being granted in certain cases,—and then they were to be open to examination and objection by all those whom the Board of Trade considered entitled to be heard. After having heard the evidence and formulated its classification and schedule of rates, the Board of Trade was instructed to endeavor to come to an agreement upon these with the railway companies. Should no agreement be arrived at, the Board of Trade was itself to determine what was "just and reasonable," and to embody this in a report. This report was to be presented to Parliament, and after the lapse of a recess the proposals contained in this report were to be submitted to Parliament in the form of Provisional Order Bills. No agreement could be arrived at between the Board of Trade and the railways. "Everybody was dissatisfied," and the board adopted the course prescribed in the Act. This inquiry was held in 1889-90 by Lord Balfour of Burleigh and Mr. (now Sir) Courtenay Boyle, on behalf of the Board of Trade, in the Westminster Town Hall. The inquiry lasted for eighty-five days; and an enormous mass of evidence, filling eleven volumes, was received. The report to the secretary of the Board of Trade by the two gentlemen named constituted the classification and schedule which they recommended as "fair and reasonable." This classification and schedule were afterwards embodied in a set of Provisional Orders. Although the classification was uniform, and the schedules of rates were nearly, though not quite alike, each railway company was legislated for by a separate Provisional Order Bill. These Provisional Order Bills were then presented to Parliament. They were not promoted by the Board of Trade, but were held to follow upon the act of 1888. After passing the second reading, they were remitted to a Joint Committee of the House of Lords and the House of Commons; and in the inquiry before that committee the whole subject was threshed out once more. The committee sat for forty-two days, and heard counsel and evidence upon all the points, and made several important amendments to the bills. Finally, the bills reappeared in Parliament, where they were further amended; * and after three years of close discussion the revised classification and rates became law on July 24, 1891, although the changes were not to take effect until August 1, 1892.†

II.

My purpose now will be to attempt to disentangle from the enormous mass of evidence some illustrations of the chief among the contested points in the theory of railway rates.

It seems necessary to say a preliminary word about the manner in which the Board of Trade and the Joint Committee of 1891 have conducted this inquiry, and have carried into effect the conclusions at which they have arrived.

Whatever may be the opinion as to the effectiveness of the legislative fixation of maximum rates or as to the advisability on abstract grounds of control over private enterprises being intrusted to government departments, no one who watched the course of the three years of controversy from 1888 till 1891 could fail to be impressed with the acuteness and fairness with which both the Joint Committee and the Board of Trade approached the subject, as well as with the comprehensiveness and thoroughness of their examination of it. The revision of the maximum rates was a work which could be expected to bring no gratitude. The railways were certain to be dissatisfied, if the traders were pleased; and, if some traders were pleased, others were certain to be dissatisfied. The arbiters among the rival interests were likely to offend them all.

* *Hansard*, Series III., vol. 356, cols. 269 *et seq.*
† The date was afterwards extended to January 1, 1893.

It is quite certain, nevertheless, that the method of re-vision of maximum rates has had a fair trial. The issue may be unfortunate from causes external to the railway system pure and simple, or from some inherent defect in the principle, or from lack of judgment or temper on the part of the railway managers or the traders; but it is unlikely that any more impartial investigation into the special conditions applicable to railway rates in England will be undertaken in our time.

Although railway companies frequently quarrel with each other,* when the question is one of demand for general reduction of rates, they stand together. Traders, on the other hand, are unaccustomed to united action. Their interests, as opposed to those of the railway com-panies, although in a superficial view identical, are really very divergent. It is the interest of the large trader to get low rates for truck-loads or for train-loads, whereas it appears to be the interest of the small trader to prevent the large trader from getting differential rates for large quantities. It is to the advantage of the trader who sends his goods to a distant market to obtain low rates, while the small trader with whom he is competing in the distant market looks upon low long-distance rates as an evil. It is to the advantage of certain traders in timber to have their goods charged by weight, while for other traders in the same commodity it is an advantage to have them charged by measurement. It is to the advantage of some traders to have a system of charges which involves de-tailed specification of charge, since an individual trader may prefer to render for himself some of the services which a railway company customarily renders; while others object to specific charges as being equivalent to an

* The time of the Railway Commissioners is largely occupied with the quarrels of railway companies. In 1886, 11 out of 12 cases before them were cases of railway against railway; in 1887, 6 out of 12; in 1889, 3 out of 11; in 1890, 7 out of 28; and, in 1891, 1 out of 19. *Annual Reports of the Railway and the Railway and Canal Commission* for these years.

attempt to extort additional rates. Here is a sufficient
divergence of interests at the outset to puzzle the most
benign and patient tribunal. Behind these more or less
reasonable differences of opinion were various forms of
unreasonable demands. It was obvious that a series of
compromises must be effected; and it was equally obvious
that, on any principle of averaging, some must be levelled
up if others were to be levelled down. These considerations did not at first enter into the representations of the
traders. Revision of rates must mean for them reduction
of rates: revised classification must mean that "no article
should be rated higher than it is at present." * Lord Balfour of Burleigh truly remarked that a classification and
schedule would have to be devised which would "satisfy
the most unreasonable of unreasonable people."

It is not easy to find any definite principle which the
Board of Trade consistently followed either in the classification or in the schedule of rates. Sometimes it would
appear as though the principle of "what the traffic would
bear," and sometimes as though "cost of service," were
the basis. What was really done was to take the clearing-house classification and the existing maximum rates,
and deal with them in a purely empirical fashion. The
principle adopted was avowedly, and perhaps under the
circumstances unavoidably, the rule of thumb.† It is the
general method of English legislation to effect a series
of compromises without troubling about consistency in
underlying theories.

As the Board of Trade conceived its duties, three
things had to be done: "(1) The codification and reduction into order of the immense mass of scattered provi-

* "First Principle of Classification," in the statement made on behalf of
the British Iron Trade Association. *Board of Trade Inquiry*, March 12, 1890,
Statement, etc., London [1890], p. 19.

† Mr. Courtenay Boyle, statement for the Board of Trade. *Report from
the Joint Select Committee of the House of Lords and House of Commons on the
Railway Rates and Charges Provisional Order Bills*, 1891.

sions relating to the charging powers of the companies; *
(2) the revision of the existing maximum charges; and
(3) it was necessary in respect to some matters, particu-
larly terminals, that charges which had not previously
been fixed and defined should for the future be fixed and
defined." † The intention of the Board of Trade was
therefore to simplify the existing complexity of rates,
and to make exhaustive specifications of what the railway
companies might charge.

This was the interpretation the Board of Trade put
upon the instructions of the Act of 1888. The railway
companies argued, or seemed to argue, that the sole duty
of the Board of Trade was codification, while the traders
seemed to argue that the sole duty of the Board was reduction of rates.

III.

A commentary on the principal points which emerged
in the course of these prolonged discussions falls naturally into the following heads: —

A. THE DEMAND FOR SPECIFICATION OF THE INGRE-
DIENTS OF CHARGE.

B. TERMINAL CHARGES: (a) Station terminals; (b)
Service terminals.

C. CONVEYANCE CHARGES: (a) Use of road; (b)
Use of locomotive power; (c) Use of wagons.

D. CLASSIFICATION: (a) As regards conveyance
charges; (b) As regards terminal charges.

---

* "They had to codify about 1,200 Acts of Parliament." Mr. Stanhope, in
the House of Commons. *Hansard*, July 24, 1891. This, however, does not by
any means represent the extent of the English Acts regulating the railway
companies. The London & North-Western Railway Company, *e.g.*, had its
Acts codified by a parliamentary barrister about ten years ago. At that time
the company was working under upwards of 1,000 Acts, including, of course,
all the Acts of the subsidiary lines which it had absorbed.

† Mr. Muir Mackenzie, statement for Board of Trade. *Provisional Order
Bills Report*, 1891, Part I., p. 16.

A. The demand for specification of the ingredients of charge appears continually in the traders' arguments, and is indeed mildly admitted by the railway companies.* The ground of the demand is that the trader ought to know for what he is paying and how much he is paying for it. There may be some part of the service which the railway company offers which he is prepared to render for himself; but he does not know whether it is worth while to do so, unless he can ascertain exactly what the railway company is charging for the particular service in question.

In order to understand conditions which have not sprung into existence in a day, but have their roots in the past, one must continually refer to ancient history; and Mr. Justice Wills was indubitably right when he said that "the notion of the railway being a highway for the common use of the public, in the same sense that an ordinary highway is so, lies at the starting-point of English railway legislation."† This notion underlies the Acts of 1845‡ and 1873§ alike. It underlies the provision in the latter Act by which the company is obliged to give details of rate;§ and it has also formed the ground of various decisions of the Railway Commissioners ‖ and of the law courts.¶ The intention of the Act of 1888** was clearly to emphasize this historical provision. The reason for the maintenance of a provision which to some seems archaic is very obvious, when we consider the English railway situation. The Midland and North-Eastern Railway Com-

---

* As, e.g., by Mr. Bidder, Q.C., for the railway companies. *Provisional Order Bills Report*, 1891, Part I., p. 70.

† *Law Reports, Queen's Bench Division* (1884–85), vol. xv. p. 530.

‡ 8 & 9 *Vict.*, c. 20, §§ 86–111.   § 36 & 37 *Vict.*, c. 48, § 14.

‖ *E.g., Thirteenth Report Railway Commissioners* (1886), pp. 6 and 30.

¶ *E.g., Hall* v. *London, Brighton & South Coast Railway, L. R., Q. B. D.*, vol. xv. p. 530.

** Sect. 33. *Cf.* also Mr. Courtenay Boyle's statement. *Provisional Order Bills Report*, 1891, Part I., p. 227.

panies are practically the only English companies which own their own mineral trucks.* The mineral trucks on other lines are almost entirely owned by traders. Again, some traders do not use the stations of the companies, but have sidings of their own, which they are entitled to have if they choose to pay for them; and, having paid for sidings, they do not expect to be called upon to pay also for the stations which they do not use. Such traders clearly want, and of course have had, as matter of practice, rates lower than the total rates, which included services of which they did not avail themselves. Another equally important reason for specification of charge lies in the circumstance that, as regards general merchandise, the English railways are not alone "conveyers" of goods, but are also "carriers"; that is, they undertake the business of "common carriers," — they collect and deliver. It may or may not be convenient or desirable that the trader should intrust the collection and delivery of his goods to the railway company; and, if he does not do so, it is argued that he ought not to be charged for a service which is not performed for him.

The extent to which this splitting up of rates may usefully be carried was actively discussed during the controversy; and the view adopted by the Board of Trade was that the splitting up should be carried out exhaustively, so that there should be no room for any other charges than those specified. The traders also desired that a clear and broad line should be drawn as to what charges the railway company may legally make.†

There were thus two elements in this demand for speci-

---

* The latter company has owned all its mineral trucks for many years; but the former only began the policy of acquiring trucks in 1881, when 60,000 or 70,000 trucks were purchased from the traders on the system at a cost of about $9,000,000. See *Report* above quoted, pp. 251, 252, and 258, Queries 1179 and 1195.

† Mr. Woodfall for the Marquis of Bute as trader. *Provisional Order Bills Report*, 1891, Part I., p. 70.

fication of charges. One was that a specific charge should *~ Mavor* be made for each individual service, and the other that these charges should be fixed, and not be subject to fluctuation. Here a curious question emerged. It was clear that, if the charge was to be fixed under the Provisional Order of the Board of Trade, the trader might be at the mercy of the Board, since at that particular stage of the proceedings the *quantum* of none of the charges was fixed. It was therefore proposed, in several instances of this specification, to provide for an appeal to arbitration, the arbitration to be conducted by a nominee of the Board *where?* of Trade. Here, however, the railway companies stepped in, and said: "No! If the charge is to be fixed, it must be fixed now. We will not submit to the arbitration of the Board of Trade." Sometimes the railways gained their point, and sometimes the traders; and thus on certain charges there is an appeal to the Board of Trade, and on certain others there is not. The traders, indeed, as subsequent proceedings have shown, have had their bugbear, "vagueness," banished at a price. *onward*

The publication of rates is a debated point upon which no definite provision is made in the bill, or, at all events, no provision other than that of previous Acts, which in this respect have not invariably been observed. The motion that the railway companies should exhibit at their stations all the actual rates chargeable from those stations was not accepted by the committee. Mr. Acworth has scouted this idea on the ground that such exhibition would require a forest of timber; but he has himself made the valuable suggestion that changes in the rates should be published in the monthly journal issued by the Board of Trade,* as the rates on the French railways are published in the *Moniteur*. The trader may, however, under the Act of 1888, demand an exhaustive analysis of his

* *Nineteenth Century*, vol. xxxi. p. 149.

rate, * so that he may, if he pleases, perform for himself any one of the services charged for.†

B.   When the railway companies promoted their bills, in 1884–85, to place the legality of terminal charges beyond question, the traders vehemently opposed them, because the proposals were unaccompanied by any modification of rates.   When the Board of Trade proposed to deal with rates and terminals together, the railways were up in arms.‡   When, however, the traders and the railway companies came face to face with the Board of Trade, in 1889, they were both obliged to give way.   The traders had to submit to terminals, and the railway companies had to submit to the " confiscatory policy " of revision of maximum rates.   The definite provision of a charge for terminals followed, indeed, logically upon the demand for specified ingredients of charge.   Under the former Acts " the rate for ' conveyance ' was the only sum which was set out in definite figures.   The sums which might be charged for station and service terminals were left vague." §   Terminals were, however, charged, ‖ although there were no statutory powers to charge specific sums for them ; and the railway companies were ever doubtful until the decision in Hall's case ¶ settled the question.

In pursuance of the policy of exhaustive specification

* Sect. 33, subsections 3 and 7.

† Since the Act, with its attendant Provisional Order Confirmation Acts of 1891 and 1892, came into force, some of the railway companies have, it would appear, refused to render the details of rates to traders.   In order to affirm the state of the law on the point, the Board of Trade took in June, 1893, the opinion of counsel.   This opinion was as follows : —
"Upon a proper application being made under subsection 3 of Section 33 of the act of 1888, the company are bound to dissect the *actual* charge made, on the ground that the subsection applies not only to the maximum rates, but also to the charge made or claimed."   *Hansard*, Series IV., vol. 12, col. 1045.

‡ See above ; and *cf.* Grierson, *Railway Rates*, p. 80.

§ *Provisional Order Bills Report*, 1891, Part II., p. 1075.

‖ *Ibid.*, p. 1112.   ¶ Quoted above.

of charge, the Board of Trade for the first time recognized
a distinction, which has now become a statutory distinction, between station terminals and service terminals.*
The meaning of this distinction is obvious. Station
terminals are charges for the use of station buildings or
sidings, while service terminals are charges for certain
manual operations.

Latin ! The pros€ and cons of the complicated question of
station terminals cannot be fully given here, but the chief
points may be suggested. In the first place, since some
traders use the station and some do not, it is clear that,
unless there were a definite reduction to the trader who
did not use the station, he would be paying for a service
which he did not demand. Moreover, unless there were
specific rates minus the terminal, no trader could tell
whether or not the rate paid by his neighbor, who loaded
his goods at his own siding, fell within the law of undue
preference. Again, if the terminal were included in the
mileage rate, the long-distance traffic might be handicapped in relation to the short-distance traffic, though
not necessarily. On the other hand, if the same terminal
were charged irrespective of distance, as was the case in
the Board of Trade schedule and is now in the Acts em-
bodying the Provisional Orders, the short-distance traffic
would be handicapped in relation to the long-distance
traffic. It happens that the kind of traffic which is most
affected is the export traffic; and it was therefore argued
that the proposed terminal would act as a restraint upon
exports. Again, it was shown that terminal facilities
varied very much, and that a uniform charge for these
would be unfair. The strongest argument, however,
against terminals was the argument that the schedule of
the Board of Trade prescribed differential distance rates
for conveyance, and that these secured for the company
due payment in respect of the circumstance that short-

* *Provisional Order Bills Report*, 1891, Part II., p. 67.

distance traffic was relatively more expensive to deal with than long-distance traffic.

(*a*) The meaning of station terminal is expressed in the following definition: "The maximum station terminal is the maximum charge which the Company may make to a trader for the use of the accommodation provided, and for the duties undertaken by the Company for which no other provision is made in this schedule, at the terminal station for or in dealing with merchandise, as carriers thereof before or after conveyance." * This definition must be taken in connection with the specification of services under service terminals. It is held to exclude specific charges for such services or duties as signalling, marshalling trucks, etc., which are held to be part of the necessary functions of the railway,† not susceptible of being made the subjects of independent charge.

(*b*) Service terminals are defined as consisting of (1°) loading, (2°) unloading, (3°) covering, and (4°) uncovering. Each of these is subject of separate charge, when separation of charge is required; and no one of them may be charged unless the service is rendered.‡

Prior to 1845 very few of the railway companies did the business of carriers,§ and thus the question of terminal charges did not arise until after the railway system had developed to some extent. Terminal charges without specification came afterwards. It was only in the schedule of 1891, constructed by the Board of Trade, that, in obe-

* *Analysis of the Railway Rates and Charges Order Confirmation Acts,* 1891 *and* 1892. Parl. Paper C.—6832, p. 102.

† For which probably they may be held to receive remuneration as "conveyers," although this special point has not been fully tested.

‡ In Class C, for example, the following are the charges: maximum station terminals, 1*s.* per ton at each end ; maximum service terminals,— (*a*) loading, 3*d.* per ton; (*b*) unloading, 3*d.* per ton; (*c*) covering, 1*d.* per ton; (*d*) uncovering, 1*d.* per ton. *Provisional Order Bills Report,* 1891, Part I., p. 154.

§ *Cf.* Mr. Littler, Q.C., in *Hall* v. *London, Brighton & South Coast Railway,* L. R., Q. B. D., vol. xv. p. 528.

dience to the principle of exhaustive dissection of charge, the separation between station and service terminals was made for the first time. * It is true that the four services detailed, with the services of collection and delivery which are now by implication excluded from terminal services in the legal sense,† were mentioned in the Act of 1873,‡ and traders were entitled to demand revision of them; but there was no provision for specification of charge such that the trader could determine whether or not he could perform any one of the services for himself more efficiently or more economically than the railway company was prepared to do it for him. Here, however, an important legal point arose. Had the trader a right to demand access to the premises of the railway company for any purpose whatever? Under the Act of 1854 the trader is entitled to "reasonable facilities"; § but it is open to doubt how far this provision will entitle him to insist upon performing services customarily performed by the railway companies. The Lancashire and Cheshire Conference proposed to the committee to make the powers definite, reserving powers to the railway companies to make by-laws; but this suggestion was not adopted.‖

While arbitration by the Board of Trade is applicable to station terminals, it is not applicable to service terminals. The attitude of both traders and of railway companies towards arbitration is curiously varied. When it is thought that arbitration will be an advantageous provision for either party, it is argued by the other that it

---

* *Provisional Order Bills Report*, 1891, Part I., p. 67.

† Collection and delivery and also weighing may be charged a reasonable sum, to be determined in case of dispute by an arbitrator appointed by the Board of Trade at the instance of either party. *Order Confirmation Acts*, London & North-Western Railway, 1891; *e.g.*, clause 5.

‡ Sect. 15.

§ Compare Mr. Pope's statement, *Provisional Order Bills Report*, 1891, Part I., p. 146, with Mr. Balfour Browne's at p. 155.

‖ *Ibid.*, p. 143.

would be very absurd to fix immutably a·charge which might, under certain conditions, come to be quite unreasonable; or it is argued that arbitration establishes no principle, and that it costs nearly as much as legal process. The railway companies accepted the principle of arbitration so far as station terminals were concerned, but objected to it for service terminals. They demanded and obtained power of "absolute charge" not changeable by arbitration.*

C. Although there is no legal definition of "conveyance," † the charges for conveyance are held in the English railway system to be composed of the following ingredients: ‡ ·(a) toll for the use of the road; § (b) haulage rates, or the payment for the use of the locomotive for haulage; and (c) payment for the use of wagons. The splitting up of rates into their constituents was much insisted upon by the traders. It was regarded as a great advantage to them.‖ This reaffirmed statutory power in the hands of the trader to demand analysis of his rate has been one of the immediate causes of the recent friction between the railways and the traders.¶

(a) First, in regard to *tolls*. Although the apparent

* Cf. *Provisional Order Bills Report*, 1891, Part I., p. xv, and Part II., p. 1114.

† See, however, Wills, J., judgment in *Hall* v. *London, Brighton & South Coast Railway*, L. R., Q. B. D., vol. xv. p. 505. See also *Provisional Order Bills Report*, 1891, Part I., pp. 34, 37, 91, and 117. "Conveyance" and "carriage" are not synonymous. The mileage rate provides for that part of the duty which is conveyance, and the station terminal (and the service terminal) for another part of the duty which is performed by the railway companies as "carriers." Cf. Mr. Bidder, Q.C., *Ibid.*, p. 75.

‡ *Report*, 1891, pp. 56 and 479. See also Grierson, *Railway Rates, English and Foreign*, 1886, pp. 96, 97.

§ Signalling is probably included in this, although the point has not been legally tested. On the traders' fear that signalling might be made the subject of a separate charge, see *Provisional Order Bills Report*, 1891, Part I., p. 82.

‖ *Provisional Order Bills Report*, 1891, Part I., p. 92.

¶ Although the power is not novel.

intention of Parliament was to deal with the whole subject of railway rates in the Act of 1888, it was accepted as
certain by the Board of Trade that, under the terms of
the Act, while it was empowered to deal with rates and
charges, it was not empowered to deal with tolls.[*] This
defect in the drafting of the Act, if it was a defect in
drafting, produced the curious result that, if the railway
companies were dissatisfied with the revised classification
and schedule,— that is, if the reduction of rates were
carried too far,— it was open to them to refuse to act as
conveyors or carriers, and simply to fall back upon their
function as road-owners and upon their statutory powers
to levy certain tolls for the exercise of that function.† If
the maximum rates and charges permitted to them by
Parliament for the total of their services fell short of their
powers of charge for one of these services, it might become their interest to follow this course. Such a policy
would result in the development of haulage companies
and of wagon companies, express companies, etc., such
as are common in America, in order to undertake functions presently performed by the railway companies.‡
The railway companies maintained, and the contention
was not rebutted by the opposing counsel, that the old
Acts of Parliament were not repealed by the Act of 1888
and the subsequent Provisional Orders, excepting in so

---

* *Provisional Order Bills Report*, 1891, Part I., p. 119; also Mr. Courtenay
Boyle's statement, p. 479.

† *Provisional Order Bills Report*, 1891, Part I., p. 118; also Grierson, *Railway Rates, English and Foreign*, 1886, p. 97.

‡ The private use of railway lines on payment of tolls is not unknown. See
Powell-Duffryn case, quoted *Provisional Order Bills Report*, 1891, Part I., p.
120. The Court of Chancery decided in this case that the only difficulty in the
way of private persons running trains over a railway line is that such persons
cannot compel the railway company to work the signals,— not because they
cannot require this to be done, but because in the nature of the case they are
not in a position to see that their orders are carried out. Some traders seem
not indisposed to attempt to frighten the railway companies by suggesting
that private companies might establish stations and charge lower terminals
than the railways. Cf. *Ibid.*, p. 264.

far as they fixed *rates and charges*, the *tolls* being left
untouched.* Saving, however, this "last trench" of the
railway companies, the old tolls were practically abolished;
and conveyance rates, including them as one of three ingredients, were substituted.

(*b*) In considering the second ingredient, *haulage rates*,
it is to be observed that the principle adopted in the
earlier English railway Acts for the fixation of maximum
tolls was the principle of "equal mileage." This arrange-
ment was drawn from the canal regulations, and also from
the fixed tolls of the horse railways which preceded the
locomotive lines; but the development of traffic produced
differential rates, and was accelerated by them. There
are two leading points in the discussion of haulage rates
in the English system. These are: (1) the graduation
of rates for distance, with or without a minimum of
chargeable distance; (2) the graduation of rates for tonnage, with or without a minimum of weight, varying with
the classification. On both of these points there is a cross-
current of interests. The interest of all large traders is
to reduce the powers of charge for quantities; and that
of some large traders, those dealing in goods which are
customarily transported to a distance, is to reduce long-
distance rates. On the other hand, it is the interest of
small traders† to prevent the large trader from having
the advantage over him which would be secured by a
differential rate in respect of quantity; and it would be
the interest of traders, large or small, whose traffic is

* Mr. Bidder, Q.C. *Provisional Order Bills Report*, 1891, Part I., p. 478.

† Or appears to be; for, if the railway company makes a large net profit
on a large wholesale traffic at a low rate, it will be able to charge lower rates
for small quantities than would be possible if its net profit were reduced, owing
to the restriction of the wholesale traffic to the goods which could afford to
pay a high rate. The effect of a differential tariff in respect of quantity
would, however, be to restrict the small trader to a purely local market. He
could not compete against the large trader in a distant market, since the
difference in rates of carriage in respect of quantity might suffice to give the
large trader a profit.

mainly local, to oppose a differential distance tariff. The railway companies' interest lies in obtaining both the highest maximum powers and permission to give differential rates in so far as these might be necessary to secure paying traffic. The railway companies' interests thus coincide at a certain point with those of both small and large traders.

(1) *Differential Rates in Respect of Distance.*— Such rates may be calculated by two methods: (*a*) by simple gradation,— so much for 10 miles, 20 miles, 50 miles, and so on; or (*b*) by the cumulative method,— so much per mile for the first 10 miles, so much less for the next 20 miles, so much less for the next 50 miles, and so on. The first method is open to the objection that the charge for, say, 19 miles will be positively greater than the charge for 21 miles, unless the reduction at each stage is infinitesimally small. This objection was surmounted by the "overlapping clause," which prescribed that the rate for one distance was not in any case to be less than the rate for a shorter distance. This method, with the overlapping clause as a rider, was the method of the English system prior to 1892. Now, however, under the new regulations, the second, or cumulative, method has been adopted, which is free from the objection of overlapping, although for long distances it involves some calculation. Given the expediency of differentiation of rate in terms of distance, there seems little to object to it on grounds of principle:

The question of minimum chargeable distance is necessarily associated with the question of terminals. Terminals are not chargeable on Class A (heavy goods); and on such goods it appeared to the Board of Trade fair to give a relatively high minimum of distance, for the reason that the cost to the railway for a short haul was greater than the amount yielded by the conveyance rate on a mileage basis pure and simple.* In this concession to

* *Provisional Order Bills Report*, 1891, Part I., p. 290.

the "cost of service" principle the Board of Trade followed precedents as well in connection with the same matter as in connection with additional mileage allowances for tunnels, etc.,— as, *e.g.*, the Severn Tunnel,— and for bridges,— as, *e.g.*, the Forth Bridge.

The older Acts gave a minimum chargeable distance of 6 miles for heavy goods conveyed at low rates; but the more recent Acts had slightly increased the maximum conveyance rate, and had given a minimum chargeable distance of 3 miles.* The new regulations give a minimum chargeable distance where no terminal is charged of 6 miles, where one terminal is charged 4½ miles, and where two terminals are charged 3 miles.† There is a proviso to the effect that, where goods pass from one line to another in the course of a journey within the minimum applicable to the class, they are not liable to a double short-distance charge.‡

The larger proportion of the traffic on the English lines is short-distance traffic.§ The average journey in the South Wales coal region is 20 miles.‖ In the Stour Valley district 35 per cent. of the traffic is transported for distances under 6 miles.¶ A vivid illustration of the mode in which short-distance traffic is conducted in England is given by Sir Henry Oakley, manager of the Great Northern Railway. "Here is a particular train upon a particular morning. It starts with 6 cars. At the first station it stops at it puts off 1 and takes on 4, at the next it puts off 3 and takes on 3, at the next it puts off 1 and takes on nothing, and at the next it puts off 6 and takes on 3, and it goes on over a journey of 76 miles. By working traffic between stations on that 76 miles, and collecting through traffic, it lands with 25 wagons at the

* *Provisional Order Bills Report*, 1891, Part I., pp. 287, 296.

† *Ibid*, p. 313.　　　　　　　‡ *Ibid.*, pp. 321, 322.

§ *Report*, Part II., p. 1126, Query 10325.

‖ *Report*, Part I., p. 249, Query 1167.　　　¶ *Ibid.*, p. 293.

end, the greatest weight it has ever had on the whole
journey." * The railway companies profess that the short-
distance traffic does not pay.† The bulk of the short-distance traffic consists of minerals,—coal and iron ore, for
example, from the pit-mouth to the iron works, or, in the
case of the former, for shipment coastwise or for export.‡
The remainder of the short-distance traffic is of the sort
described above. § Some of this traffic, especially on
branch lines, is probably often conducted in an unnecessa-
rily expensive manner. ‖

According as we regard it from the point of view of the
"cost of service" or from the point of view of "what the
traffic will bear," the reduced rate per mile for the long
haul rests either upon the principle that it costs less per
mile to move a ton 100 miles than it costs to move it 10
miles, or upon the principle that the distance to which
traffic can be procured for carriage is in reciprocal proportion to the rate per mile.¶

(2) *Differential Rates in respect of Quantity.*— In the

* *Provisional Order Bills Report*, 1891, Part I., p. 309. The average speed
of these local trains is 6 miles an hour. *Ibid.*, p. 300, Query 1401.

† " It has forced itself upon our minds constantly that, practically, the
long-distance traffic pays for the extra expenses incurred in working the short-
distance traffic. We must get a dividend ; and, if we cannot get it out of the
short distances, we must get it out of the long distances." Manager of Great
Northern Railway in evidence, *Provisional Order Bills Report*, 1891, Part I.,
p. 309, Query 1529.

‡ The extent to which the mineral traffic pays or does not pay is a disputed
point. *Cf.* the rival views of Mr. Conder, *Proceedings Institution of Mechanical
Engineers* (England), 1878, p. 184, and of Mr. Price Williams, *Ibid.*, 1879, p.
96. *Cf.* also observations on the relative profit of passenger and goods traffic.
Statement British Iron Trade Association [1890], p. 16.

§ Shunting heavy traffic is said to cost on the London & North-Western
Railway Company 11.6 per cent. of the entire cost of locomotive power used on
the line. *Proceedings Institution of Mechanical Engineers*, 1878, p. 187.

‖ See the remarks of Mr. Bergeron, *Ibid.*, 1879, p. 147 ; and *cf.* Herbert
Spencer's criticism, " Railway Morals and Railway Policy," *Essays*, p. 301.

¶ From the point of view of railway administration both principles must be
taken into account. Cf. *Atti della Commissione d' Inchiesta sull' Exercizio delle
Ferrovie Italiane*, 1884, Parte II., vol. ii. p. 957 *et seq.*

earlier Acts there was no minimum of quantity. There were equal tonnage rates within the class; and the class was fixed with exclusive regard to the nature of the goods, irrespective of quantity.* Under the railway clearing-house classification the minimum of weight was fixed at 4 tons for goods heavy in relation to their value per unit of weight, and at 2 tons for light goods.† This limitation grew up in practice within the maximum total rates.‡ There are two elements in the fixation of the minimum quantity: (1) the minimum quantity consignable at a certain rate, and (2) the minimum load at a certain rate. That these elements are distinct § will be obvious when one considers that the same trader — a chemical manufacturer, for example — might send in one consignment separate packages of different goods which could not be loaded in the same ~~truck~~ _wagon_ without danger. Such goods are subjected to a provision for a minimum load independently of the provision for a minimum consignment.‖ The increasing size of the ~~trucks~~ _wagons_ in use on the railway system rendered such provisions necessary from the railway point of view;¶ and the large traders demanded concessions in rates in consideration of large consignments. These large traders, whose business required relatively small consignments, together with the small traders, objected to a high minimum of weight at a certain rate, because they were unable to take advantage of the reduction by consigning in large quantities. It happened that the agricultural interest was involved in this question, not

* " In no important act is there any limit of consignment for tonnage rate." Mr. Courtenay Boyle, _Provisional Order Bills Report_, 1891, Part I., p. 503.

† _Provisional Order Bills Report_, 1891, Part I., p. 497 _et seq._

‡ _Ibid._, p. 503.   § _Ibid._, p. 504.

‖ These are in Class 10. _Ibid._, pp. 504 and 510.

¶ In 1860 the largest truck had a capacity of 6 tons, in 1891 of 10 tons. _Provisional Order Bills Report_, 1891, Part I., p. 510, Queries 3475 and 3476. See also _Proceedings of Institution of Mechanical Engineers_, 1884, p. 416. "The average daily load of goods trucks does not exceed one-half." _Ibid._, p. 431.

so much because agricultural produce was usually sent in
lots of less than 4 tons,— for, as it happened, the consignments usually exceeded that quantity,* — but because
artificial manures were customarily sent in lots of 2 tons
and under 4 tons.† There were also many products
of iron manufacture which came in the same category
as chemical manures in this respect. These interests prevailed at the Board of Trade inquiry, and the minimum
consignment in the heavy class at a low rate was fixed
at 2 tons.‡ But this did not satisfy the railway companies nor the large traders,§ and they succeeded in in-
ducing the committee to raise the minimum from 2 to
4 tons.‖ Perhaps the chief consideration which weighed
with the committee was that the railway companies had
reduced actual rates for long-distance traffic on the basis
of a 4-ton limit, and that reduction to a 2-ton limit
might weaken the argument for maximum rates approxi-
mating to the existing actual rates. The differential
rate as finally adjusted follows the classification. Heavy
goods are charged according to the rate in Class A, if
they are in 4-ton lots; according to Class B, if in lots of
less than 4 tons; and in Class C, if in lots of less than 2
tons.¶ Apart from the inferior limit of consignment,
there is the question of graduated rates for quantities.
The Board of Trade proposed to divide heavy traffic into
three divisions as regards weight of consignment: (1)
consignments under 10 tons; (2) those between 10 and

* *Provisional Order Bills Report*, 1891, Part I., p. 510, Query 3470.

† *Ibid.*, p. 504.   ‡ *Ibid.*, p. 487 *et seq.*   § *Ibid.*, p. 488.

‖ *Ibid.*, p. xxxi.   ¶ *Ibid.*, pp. 530 and 540; also p. xxxii.

NOTE.—In England the goods ton is 2,240 pounds, and the mineral ton is
2,352 pounds. In America the ton is 2,000 pounds. The ratio of American to
English weights is thus 1 to 1.12 and 1 to 1.176 for goods and minerals re-
spectively. These important differences are generally overlooked in attempts
to compare rates.

250 tons; (3) those above 250 tons.* These figures were employed to define precisely the indefinite expressions "truck-load" and "train-load." But the traders . in 4-ton consignments now united with the traders in smaller consignments to defeat the 10 to 250 ton proposal, which was clearly made in the interests of the large traders.† Since, again, high maximum powers were what the railways wanted,‡ and since the railways and some of the traders united their forces, the stronger battalions were against the proposal; and so the committee were constrained to throw it out. The differentiation of rate thus existing is that indicated above in connection with minimum consignments. Having offended the small traders by fixing the minimum consignment at 4 tons, the committee propitiated them by rejecting the train-load proposal of the Board of Trade.§

(c) The third ingredient of the conveyance rate is the payment for the use of the ~~wagon~~. The clause dealing with this point, as finally adjusted, states that in cases where the railway company do not provide trucks "the charge authorized for conveyance shall be reduced by a reasonable sum, which shall, in case of difference between the company and the person liable to pay the charge, be determined by an arbitrator to be appointed by the Board

---

* *Provisional Order Bills Report*, 1891, Part II., p. 1075. As regards the 10 and 250 ton gradation, the reduction of rate applies only to Classes A and B; as regards the 10-ton gradation (the second division), it applies only to Classes C and 1. *Ibid.*

† There were alleged to be only 6 or 7 coal-traders in London who could deal with train-loads. *Ibid.*, p. 1138, Query 10601. For the arguments of the large traders, see *Statement British Iron Trade Association* [1890], p. 18.

‡ The railway companies denied that there was any material difference in cost between handling traffic in truck-loads collected from several different traders and handling traffic in train-loads forwarded by individual traders. Some colliery owners agreed with this view. *Provisional Order Bills Report*, 1891, Part II., Query 10211; also Query 10756.

§ *Provisional Order Bills Report*, 1891, p. xlix.

of Trade." * The provision of trucks is not obligatory
upon the railway in respect of Class A and certain other
selected goods in Class B,—lime, for instance. In the
older Acts the charge for wagon hire was not invariably
specified; but, where specified, it was, as a rule, one-
eighth of a penny (⅛ cent) per ton per mile.† The
traders were exceedingly anxious to have this portion of
the dissected rate definitely fixed.‡ Some urged that it
should be fixed at one-half the rate mentioned.§ But
the differences between one railway and another, and between one set of traders and another, were found to be so
great that the charge for wagon hire was not fixed at a
uniform specific rate; but it was held to be included in
the conveyance rate, specification to be made by the railway companies to the traders on the general principle of
specification of ingredients of rate.

The question is an exceedingly difficult and important
one; for in practice it may occur that the rate for Class
A, which is exclusive of wagon hire,—the railway companies not being obliged to provide wagons for that class,
—may, when the wagon hire is added, actually exceed
the rate for Class B, where the companies do customarily
provide the wagons. The rate of wagon hire must therefore be kept at a point below that under which this state
of charge would arise. It seemed difficult to do this ar-
bitrarily with equal justice to all the interests; and therefore, as in other cases of a similar order, the matter was
left for settlement by arbitration by the Board of Trade
in case of need.

In connection with this the following features of the

---

* *Provisional Order Bills Report*, 1891, Part I., p. 55. The number of
traders' trucks on the London & North-Western Railway system alone amounts
to 84,000, while the number of trucks owned by the railway company is only
54,550. *Railway and Canal Traffic Act*, 1888, Return in pursuance of Sect. 32,
etc., c. 5930, 1890, p. 10.

† *Provisional Order Bills Report*, 1891, Part I., p. 263.   ‡ *Ibid.*, p. 1056.

§ Statement by Mining Association of Great Britain, quoted *Ibid.*, p. 263.

English system are to be noted. The return of empty
trucks is not in present practice made the subject of a
separate charge.* The wagons of private owners or companies are subject to very great detention. A wagon
makes, for example, on an average, only two journeys
a month, when employed in traffic between the north
and the south of England.† A journey of twenty-five
miles usually takes a wagon a week to go and return.‡
The interests of the railway companies and of the wagon-
owners are, up to a certain point, identical; and then
they become divergent. It is important for both that
a relatively large charge should be made for wagon hire;
for the railways charge those who do not have wagons
the prescribed rate, while the wagon-owners get the prescribed rate by way of rebate.§ On the other hand, it
is not to the interest of the railway companies to have
the specified rate for wagons too high, otherwise the
rebate to the owners of private wagons would be excessive.‖ In consequence of the strength of the interests
of owners of wagons,— not wagon companies, but traders
carrying their own traffic in their own wagons,— a proviso was inserted, giving the owners of wagons power
to charge demurrage against the railway companies for
detention of trucks,¶ the railway companies having
similar powers of charge for detention of trucks belong-
ing to them.

D. The railway companies throughout the country
had, by common consent, adopted the classification of the

---

* *Provisional Order Bills Report*, 1891, Part I., p. 419 *et seq.* Occasionally
it happens that the railway company use these private trucks, admittedly with
or without permission. See *Ibid.*, p. 421.

† *Ibid.*, p. 246.   ‡ *Ibid.*, p. 251.

§ Compare *Report from the Joint Committee of the House of Lords and the
House of Commons on the Railway Rates and Charges Provisional Order Bills*,
1891, Part I., p. 160.

‖ *Ibid.*, p. 242.   ¶ *Ibid.*, p. 209.

Railway Clearing House. This classification had no statutory force. It simply embodied the customs of the trade. It had not been made: it had grown. There were 4,000 specified articles, and the recognized plan of altering rates was to move the article in which the change was to take place from one class to another.* The railway clearing-house classification was therefore subject to constant change. Lord Balfour of Burleigh and Mr. Courtenay Boyle conferred with the railway managers and the traders for thirteen days upon classification,† and the outcome was the classification proposed by the Board of Trade in the Provisional Order Bills of 1891. Although the proposed classification was based upon that of the railway clearing house, it was, necessarily, entirely different in effect. The old classification was subject to alteration from day to day, as the movements of rates demanded.‡ The new classification was immutable, at all events, without the sanction of Parliament. The first step of the Board of Trade was to reduce the number of the specified articles from 4,000 to 2,000. § The resulting classification is really entirely empirical. It is not fixed on any logical basis. Any serious change in established practice would have been open to the charge of giving particular districts or particular trades undue advantages over others.

* Cf. *The Railway and Canal Traffic Act*, 1888, by W. A. Hunter, LL.D., M.P., London, 1889, p. 82.

† Yet the traders' counsel pleaded before the Joint Committee that the classification satisfied neither party. *Provisional Order Bills Report*, 1891, Part I., p. 488.

‡ English railway rates do not fluctuate nearly so much as rates in America, while sudden and considerable changes are almost unknown. The changes following upon the legislation of 1891-92 are the most violent that have taken place in England for many years.

§ The Lancashire and Cheshire Conference, which was the exponent in general of the traders' grumbles, complained of this reduction in number of specified articles; but they did not object to the principles on which the classification had been based. *Provisional Order Bills Report*, 1891, Part I., p. 487.

The principles of classification urged by an influential body of traders * were these : —

1. That no article should be rated higher than it is at present (*i.e.*, under the railway clearing-house classification as it existed in 1890). The traders have now got a classification which should be amended, not increased.

2. Classification means liability to damage or special expense.

3. Undamageable articles should all be placed in the lowest category, which should be varied in proportion to damageability and costliness of carriage.

4. The nature of a commodity, its degree of safeness, its easiness of transit, its bulk, its quantity, and its traffic-producing qualities are the considerations that should regulate its classification.

This statement illustrates the attitude of the traders. The principles upon which the Board of Trade actually proceeded were the following : † —

(*a*) Value ; (*b*) damageability ; (*c*) risk ; (*d*) weight in proportion to bulk ; (*e*) facility for trading ; (*f*) mass of consignments ; (*g*) facility for handling.

The Board of Trade, in seeking to attain uniformity, was obliged, on one hand, to invade the privileges of the railway companies, and, on the other, to trespass upon the feelings of the traders by raising the classification of certain goods.‡ In cases of new articles arising, the Board of Trade is now empowered, under Section 24 of the Act of 1888,§ to class such articles ; but it has no power to alter the classification or the maximum rates fixed by the Provisional Order Confirmation Acts of 1891 and 1892.

In the fixation of the maximum rates, the Board of Trade applied a uniform scale to the railway companies,

* The British Iron Trade Association. See *Statement* [1890], p. 19.

† *Provisional Order Bills Report*, 1891, Part I., p. 18.

‡ The bulk of the discussion upon classification was in connection with manufactured iron. See Mr. Courtenay Boyle's statement, *Provisional Order Bills Report*, 1891, Part I., p. 612 *et seq.*

§ 51 & 52 *Vict.*, c. 25, § 24, subsection 11.

so far as seemed practicable. Yet the differences are not
unimportant. The following table exhibits the mode in
which the scale has been applied : —

MAXIMUM RATES.

I.	II.	III.
Absolutely the same.	Slightly higher than List I.	Slightly higher than List II.
L. & N. W. Ry.	Midland	Brighton
Great Western	Great Eastern	South-Western
Great Northern	—	South-Eastern
—	—	L., C. & Dover

The chief differences are in Classes A and B. In the
higher classes the rates are practically the same.*
The following tables † illustrate the differences between
the proposals of the Board of Trade, the railway companies, and the traders : —

TABLE A.

BOARD OF TRADE CUMULATIVE SCALE.

CLASS.	For first 20 miles.	For next 30 miles.	For next 50 miles.	For remainder of distance.
C	1.80d.	1.50d.	1.20d.	0.70d.
1	2.20	1.85	1.40	0.90
2	2.65	2.30	1.70	1.35
3	3.10	2.65	1.75	1.65
4	3.60	3.15	2.20	1.80
5	4.30	3.70	3.25	2.30

* Lord Balfour of Burleigh, *Provisional Order Bills Report*, 1891, Part I.,
p. 432. The terminals are uniform. See *Ibid.*, p. liv.

† From *Provisional Order Bills Report*, 1891, pp. lv, lvi.

TABLE B.

Railway Companies' Cumulative Scale.

Alleged to be the Equivalent of the Normanton Scale.

Class.	For first 20 miles.	For next 30 miles.	For next 50 miles.	For remainder of distance.
C	2.40*d.*	1.30*d.*	1.10*d.*	0.90*d.*
1	2.80	1.70	1.60	1.20
2	3.00	2.50	1.80	1.70
3	3.30	2.80	2.40	2.20
4	3.90	3.40	3.00	2.60
5	4.50	4.00	3.30	2.75

TABLE C.

Traders' Cumulative Scale.

Class.	For first 20 miles.	For next 30 miles.	For next 50 miles.	For remainder of distance.
C	1½*d.*	1¼*d.*	1*d.*	¾*d.*
1	1¾	1½	1¼	1
2	2	1¾	1½	1¼
3	2¼	2	1¾	1½
4	3	2½	2¼	2
5	3½	3	2½	2¼

The above tables contain exclusively suggested maximum "conveyance" rates.

OLD MAXIMUM RATES.*

	Per Ton per Mile.
Coal, coke, etc. (now Class A):	
Up to 50 miles	1⅛*d.*
Beyond 50 miles	⅞*d.*

*From the leading Act of the London and North-Western Railway, 1846 (9 & 10 *Vict.*, c. 204). *Cf.* also Hunter, *The Railway and Canal Traffic Act, 1888*, London, 1889, p. 142.

	Per Ton per Mile.

Heavy goods (approximately Class B) :
  Up to 50 miles . . . .   1¼d. to 1½d.
  Beyond 50 miles . . . .   1d. to 1⅛d.

Heavy goods (approximately Class C) :
  Up to 50 miles . . . .   2d.
  Beyond 50 miles . . . .   1¼d.

Higher goods (Classes 1 to 5):
  Up to 50 miles . . . .   2½d. to 3½d.
  Beyond 50 miles . . . .   2d. to 3d.

NEW MAXIMUM RATES.

CUMULATIVE SCALE PROPOSED BY BOARD OF TRADE AND NOW ADOPTED.*

Rates per Ton per Mile in Fractions of 1d. (2 cents).

	For the first 20 miles or any part of such distance.	For the next 30 miles or any part of such distance.	For the next 50 miles or any part of such distance.	For the remainder of the distance.	Station terminal at each end.
Class A, minerals, etc , exclusive of charge for trucks .	0.95d.	0.85d.	0.50d.	0.40d.	3.00d.
Class B, including trucks . .	1.60	1.20	0.80	0.50	
Class C	1.80	1.50	1.20	0.70	
Class 1	2.20	1.85	1.40	0.90	
Class 2	2.65	2.30	1.70	1.35	
Class 3	3.10	2.65	1.75	1.65	
Class 4	3.60	3.15	2.20	1.80	
Class 5	4.30	3.70	3.25	2.30	

* *Provisional Order Bills Report*, 1891, pp. 1, liv, lv.

IV.

It remains to consider the effects of the legislation of 1888–91, and afterwards the transactions which followed upon the Order Confirmation Acts coming into force.

The general effect of the new legislation has undoubtedly been to intensify the control of Parliament over the railway system. Such a revision of maximum rates as might involve a reduction of them was always strenuously opposed by the railway companies and their advocates. It was alleged that such a policy would be at once unjust and impracticable. The policy has been carried out, although the justice of it is perhaps still open to question, and the practical working of the revised scale has already produced much friction between the traders and the Board of Trade on one side and the railway companies on the other.

In detail the new legislation effects a series of compromises, and offers a series of propitiations. The small trader is propitiated by the refusal to the large trader of the benefit of a reduced rate for train-loads; while even the reduced rate for the truck-load is not so low as the large trader would like. The trader in through traffic is propitiated by the cumulative scale; while the owners of wagons and of sidings are considered in the provisions for dissecting rates, and the powers which make it possible for a trader to perform nearly all the functions of a railway company for himself if he chooses. The trader in heavy goods, coal, iron, etc. (Class A), is, on the whole, the trader most highly benefited by the new regulations. He gets a substantial reduction in rates. On the other hand, the railway companies have obtained increased powers of charge in the higher classes of goods; and they have obtained, moreover, statutory powers to charge terminals, which they had long demanded. There is no evidence so far to show that the agitation of the traders or the action of the legislature in subjecting railway companies to intensified control by the Board of Trade has had any influence in diminishing the attractiveness to the investing public of railway enterprise in England. The table on page 405 shows that the amount of capital proposed to be raised and the number of miles of railway projected have increased largely during the very period when the controversy was acutest.* It is fairly clear that the building of new railways and the investment of capital in them are determined rather by the conditions of industry than by legislative action affecting rates. The year 1889 was "a more than ordinarily prosperous year for the railway companies." † The years 1890 and 1891 were also good years. The increasing volume of trade accounts for the new enterprises; but there is no visible reason to believe that any of these were prevented from coming to maturity by the anticipation of diminished revenues following upon the adoption of the Board of Trade schedule. Since these schedules came into operation only on January 1, 1893, there is hardly yet room for other than provisional conclusions upon their effect. Their advent was nearly coincident with a falling off in trade, which has since almost steadily continued, with the result that traffic receipts are diminished from causes other than those connected with rate movements.

* Mr. Findley, of the London & North-western Railway, argued against reduction of maximum rates, on the ground that the revenue of the railway companies would be thereby "clipped," that the credit of the companies would suffer, and that they would have on this account to pay higher rates of interest upon loans. *Provisional Order Bills Report*, 1891, Part II., p. 1105, Query 10086.

† *General Report to the Board of Trade in regard to Share and Loan Capital, etc., of the Railway Companies of the United Kingdom*, for the year 1889 [C.-6157], p. 13.

NEW RAILWAY BILLS PROMOTED, 1887–90.*

	1887.	1888.	1889.	1890.
No. of bills promoted by new railway companies applying for powers . .	19	20	19	23
Length of new lines proposed by these companies in miles	142	226	331	376
Amount of new capital proposed to be raised by these companies	$41,800,000	$54,400,000	$49,400,000	$84,600,000
No. of bills promoted by existing railway companies applying for powers . .	62	82	73	91
Length of new lines proposed by these in miles .	84	220	223	399
Amount of new capital proposed to be raised by these companies . . .	$41,300,000	$66,000,000	$52,400,000	$86,600,000
Total length of new lines proposed	226	446	554	775
Total amount of capital proposed to be raised . .	$83,100,000	$120,400,00	$101,800,000	$171,200,000
Capital proposed to be raised per mile of line . {	$367,768 (£75,575)	$248,100 (£55,480)	$184,705 (£37,953)	$221,582 (£45,533)

V.

During the winter of 1892–93, immediately after the Provisional Order Confirmation Bills were passed, friction again arose between the railways and the traders. This time the railways were the aggressors. They promptly raised their rates in many cases to the maximum, and at once brought about their ears the loudest expostulations of their aggrieved customers. The companies were clearly anxious to show that maximum rates were unworkable; and the traders were bitterly disappointed at the result of the long-considered legislation. Revision had been called " confiscation " ; and the tables were turned upon the " confiscators." In consequence of the action of the

* See *Report by the Board of Trade upon all the Railway, Canal, etc., Bills of Session*, 1887; *Ibid.*, 1888; *Ibid.*, 1889; *Ibid.*, 1890.

railway companies and the loud grumbling of the traders, Sir Albert Rollit, a ship-owner and solicitor, gave notice in the House of Commons in the spring of 1893 of a motion for the appointment of a Committee of Inquiry.* This motion was withdrawn; but shortly afterwards the president of the Board of Trade (Mr. Mundella) moved the appointment of a Select Committee † to inquire into the mode in which the railway companies had exercised the powers conferred upon them in the acts confirming their Provisional Orders passed in 1891-92, and "to consider whether it is desirable to adopt any other means of settling the difficulties arising between the companies and the public with respect to the rates and conditions of charges for the conveyance of goods." ‡

This Committee met near the end of May, and continued to receive evidence until November, 1893.§

The chief points in their reports can alone be dealt with. The leading question was, Did the railway companies break faith with the public and with the Board of Trade, in raising at a stroke their actual rates to the maximum allowed by law? That the companies did raise their rates, or the greater part of them, there is no reason to doubt. They really substituted for their existing rate-books a rate-book which contained simply the new maximum rates. The possibility of some such *coup* was at least partially foreseen; and, in some cases at least, the answers of railway managers to queries made during the investigations of 1889-91 were open to the interpretation

---

* A bill to amend the Act of 1888 had been previously introduced by Mr. R. D. Burnie and others, but it was not proceeded with. Its terms were short and drastic. The companies were to be forbidden to increase rates above the actual rates in existence prior to the passing of the Acts of 1891-92, and were to be subjected to a penalty in case of their being convicted of overcharging. Bill 36, 1st of February, 1893.

† May 16, 1893. See *Hansard.* ‡ *Ibid.*

§ *First Report on Railway Rates and Charges*, 1893, No. 385; *Second Report on Railway Rates and Charges*, 1893, No. 462.

that no such *coup* was intended, or, even if intended, practicable. *

It was pointed out, *e.g.*, by Sir Henry Oakley † that the companies could "not hope to get any increase of rates by exercising any margin of power which" might be given to them, simply because such increase would damage the trade. "If we thought now that an increase would not damage the trade, we should make an addition at this moment." According to the Report of 1893,‡ "the bulk of the evidence given on behalf of the railway companies was to the same effect." The Report adds that, in deference to the representations of the railway companies to the effect that, if the rates on certain classes of goods were reduced, the companies would be obliged to recoup themselves in some way, the Joint Committee raised the maximum rates, in order to reduce the expected loss to the companies. The conclusion of the Report is that,—

The effect of the statements of the railway managers before the Board of Trade Committee and the Joint Committee of the Houses was to lead these bodies and the traders to believe, that the companies could not recoup themselves for any losses resulting from a reduction of the maximum charges by a general raising of rates which were below the maxima. If there had been any general expectation of such action, it is most probable that the provisional orders would not have passed into law; for they would have been strongly opposed by the traders who had the benefit of the existing rates, and who would have objected to their being raised for the benefit of other traders whose rates were to be reduced.

On the other hand, it was undoubtedly expected by the Board of Trade and Parliament that the companies would find it possible to make some increases in exceptionally low rates, to an extent which would partially recover their losses in other directions.

* *E.g.*, Query 5426, p. 668, *Report of* 1891; and Query 13911, p. 1453, *Report of* 1891, etc. A full list of these references will be found in the Appendix to the *Report of* 1893, No. 385.

† Query 13868, *Report of* 1891, p. 1451.   ‡ *Second Report*, No. 462, p. v.

The expediency of raising the actual rates to the maxima was anxiously discussed by the railway managers during 1892, and the decision to make the *coup* seems not to have been unanimous. They determined, however, to raise the rates in general to the maxima, on two grounds, partly in order to recoup their losses and partly because of "the difficulties of dealing with the new maxima." The railway managers complained that the time allowed between the passing of the Acts and their coming into force was too short,* and that the classification adopted by Parliament "was not detailed enough." The companies, however, appear to have intended to modify the rates to suit special cases as these arose.

While these complaints were probably not remotely connected with a desire to show that the Acts were unworkable, it is to be noted that they are complaints of details and have no ostensible bearing upon the fixation of maximum rates by Parliament, nor upon the right of Parliament to interfere where the railways suddenly advance their actual rates, even when these advanced rates come within the maxima.

The Committee observe, with some point, that they feel it "difficult to understand fully the explanations afforded by the railway companies, and still more difficult to justify what they do understand of them." The Committee also point out that there were two courses open to the railway companies: one was to issue a maximum rate-book along with an announcement that the rates were provisional, and the other to leave the actual rates as they were, excepting in cases where reduction was required by law, and afterwards to raise any exceptionally low rates by degrees. The adoption of the first course, without, however, any intimation of the provisional character of the

---

* Although some of the Acts were not passed until the summer of 1892, the London & North-western Railway Act was passed on August 5, 1891, while it did not come into force until January 1, 1893, a period of seventeen months.

rates, produced the result which might have been foreseen by the railway companies; namely, the rebellion of the traders. The Committee found that "such a course was most unsatisfactory, and that the companies were not justified in dislocating trade and alarming so many interests, and in compelling traders to enter into long negotiations with them for the revision of rates.* It was shown also that, as regards some of the railways, the gain by increased rates was far in excess of the loss by diminished ones.†

Such a policy as that adopted by the railway companies can only be judged by results. There can be no doubt that it failed, if not utterly, at least to a very large extent. The suddenness of the *coup* infuriated the customers of the railways. They withheld payment of their accounts, and the utmost friction was produced. The representations of the traders and of Parliament forced the railways to abandon the position they had taken up, and to return to the rates of 1892, with, however, an increase of 5 per cent. in those rates which were not affected by the reduction clauses, provision for special cases being made gradually. The manœuvre of the railways can thus hardly be said from a tactical point of view to have been well managed. Their action has impressed the public mind with the feeling that they cannot be trusted, and that they must be continually watched; and, more important still, it has brought up the serious question of the practicability of revising actual as well as maximum rates. Some provision for dealing with actual rates is hinted at, although none is specifically recommended in the Report of the Committee.

The most important recommendation of the Committee referred to the Railway Commission and its powers. It is recommended that the membership of the Commission should be subject to revision from time to time, that one of the members should be experienced in trade, and that

* *Report*, 1893, No. 462, p. viii.   † *Ibid.*, p. ix.

costs should not be awarded on either side unless the claim or defence has been frivolous or vexatious.*

VI.

The repeated revival of the railway rates question, and the chronic condition of inquiry in which for twenty years it has existed in almost every country, whatever may be the system of railway administration, suggest that there is some general cause for the pressure upon railway companies to reduce rates, and for their apparent inability to meet the demand to a sufficient extent. Without attempting to develop a theory of transportation, it may be suggested that the general cause, put briefly, is that, while improved transportation has contributed to the reduction of prices of goods, especially in the great market centres,† it has not similarly reduced its own price. In other words, while formerly the sale of 10 pounds of pig iron would realize enough to transport 100 pounds say 100 miles, it would now be necessary to sell 20 pounds of pig iron to transport the same quantity the same distance.‡ Transportation charges thus tend at present to form a progressively increasing proportion of the realized price. In the higher classes of goods the variation of proportion of transport cost to total cost is clearly of less importance than in the case of lower classes of goods. With these lower classes of goods, pig iron and coal, for instance, every reduction of the price, without a corresponding reduction of rate,§ means a serious increase in the ratio of transport cost to total price.

* *Report of* 1893, No. 462, p. xiii.

† *Cf.* Sax. Schönberg's *Handbuch der Pol. Oek.*, vol. i. pp. 498, 499.

‡ The figures are simply used by way of illustration.

§ This has been to some extent recognized in practice. In the north of England, where the wages sliding-scale is well known, a railway rates sliding-scale was in existence until recently (I am not aware whether or not it exists at the moment). By this sliding-scale, when pig iron falls below 45s. per ton, the rate is reduced by 1% for every 1s. per ton. Cf. *Report Commission on Depression of Trade*, p. 346, 1886, *Second Report*, Part I.

The conditions which the railways have contributed to produce have reacted upon the railways.

The fixation of maximum rates is a subsidiary question. The demand for this is due to the suspicion attaching to all monopolies and *quasi*-monopolies,— that there is an element in the price which is due to exploitation in the sinister sense. The stock list of the English railways does not, however, suggest that this element is important, or, indeed, that it exists at all. The railway rates problem might exist, even though there were no interest to be paid upon capital. If the railways were conducted on the principle of charging bare running expenses alone,* it is conceivable that in time the increased mobility of goods would result, under certain conditions, in prices so low that the transport cost would appear to be an intolerable tax. The increased mobility of goods, with all its economic and social, direct and indirect effects, must be paid for in some way.

A suggestion may be hazarded as to the reason why transport cost should remain relatively high, while prices of goods fall. The reason appears to me to be twofold: (1) The goods which the railway company buys and sells are not principally those in which prices have been diminishing. The consumption of raw material on a railway even in its construction is relatively small : the wage-bill in construction, in maintenance, and in running, is relatively large. I find that the wage-bill on one of the Scotch lines is as follows : —

Percentage to Total Expenses.		Wages.	Materials, etc.
15%	A. Maintenance of way	50%	50%
32%	B. Locomotive power	45%	55%
13%	C. Repairs and renewals . . .	30%	70%
35%	D. Traffic expenses	75%	25%
5%	E. General charges	45%	55%
100%		54%	46%

* Or if the road were free, as the Erie Canal is free.

These figures are probably fairly typical. The cost of
human service has probably, on the whole, risen in civilized
countries during the past thirty years; and this explains
in an obvious way how the cost of transport has been
maintained. (2) But perhaps a more important reason
than the first is that the law of diminishing returns has
a special application to railways. In the mechanism of
transportation the limit of possible work from a given
installation of that mechanism is reached at an early
stage, when compared with the extensive limits of possible
work from the productive mechanism of staple products.
In those industries whose mechanism is susceptible of
rapid improvement, without rendering valueless a dis-
proportionate amount of capital, the curve of production
determined by the law of diminishing returns is checked
by improvements at frequent points. But transportation
is not an industry of that sort. The mechanism of it, in
England especially, is among the most permanent orders of
mechanism. Even minor improvements are retarded by
the costly and substantial character of the railway struct-
ures. The Great Western Railway was almost obliged to
retain a gauge of line different from all the other railways
until 1892, because of the enormous cost the alteration involved. Wagons have not changed in shape or character * since George Stephenson's time, because the curves,
the gradients, the turn-tables, the coal shoots, and other
appliances would have to be altered to suit a new type of
wagon.†

The curve of cost per train mile steadily descends with
a frequency of from one to twenty trains per day over the

* *Proceedings of Institution of Mechanical Engineers*, 1890, p. 475.

† *Ibid.*, 1884, p. 441. There are, of course, other reasons why the English
railways do not adopt the American type of bogie truck. Among the chief
of these is the hilly nature of the mineral fields, so far as mineral traffic is concerned, and the smallness of the lots of goods customarily transported at a time,
so far as general merchandise is concerned.

same lines.* The limit is then reached, and with a higher
frequency the curve ascends.† Alike as regards the economical limit of speed,‡ of gradient,§ of curvature of line,‖
of size and weight of wagons,¶ of number and weight of
trains,** the railway companies are "hampered" by the
law of diminishing returns,— a piece of legislation which
has not been procured by agitating traders, nor concocted
by a Joint Committee, but which has all, and more than
all, the force of a Provisional Order. Such limitations as
have been described in the working of rolling stock, as
well as limitations in the efficiency of stations and of administration, have so great a cumulative effect upon the
railway system that the cost to it of transporting goods
does not diminish quite so fast as the cost of production of
those goods.†† If the cost of production be taken as the
inferior limit below which the market price of an article in
constant supply does not under normal conditions perma-
nently fall, then we may say that the market price of
transport is not likely to fall in so great a proportion as
the fall which has taken place in the market prices of
certain goods.

What must strike any one in studying the English railway system is the great complexity alike of conditions
and of interests,— a complexity inseparable from an ex-

* See paper by Lieutenant-Colonel Dowden. *Professional Papers on Ind-
ian Engineering*, Series III., vol. iii., No. 10, quoted in *Proceedings* of *Institution* of *Civil Engineers* (England), vol. lxxxii. p. 403.

† For American experience to the same effect, see Wellington, *The Economic Theory of Railway Location*, p. 569.

‡ See Price Williams, *Institution of Mechanical Engineers* (England), 1878, p.
202; Wellington, *op. cit.*, p. 460.

§ *Ibid.*, p. 346. ‖ *Ibid.*, p. 323.

¶ Discussion, *Institution of Mechanical Engineers* (England), 1884, p. 431.

** Wellington, *op. cit.*, p. 571.

†† This principle is probably not confined to railways. The cost of bullock
cartage in India is 6d. per ton per mile, which is perhaps a much higher rate
than prevailed thirty years ago.

tensive commerce conducted within an area relatively small, but exceedingly diversified in physical and industrial characteristics. A perfectly uniform and simple system, even if it were practicable, would probably be unjust; and thus the only way out of the *impasse* in which the railway problem seems likely to be landed is a more and more strenuous and minute study of the actual conditions under which the traffic is or might be carried on. The railway managers and the traders alike will have to abandon the crass attitude which some of them adopt.* There are probably many important economies in administration which might be effected; and thus a diminution in rates, with probable, although not certain, increase of traffic, might be made without reduction of dividends.†

The railway system has grown so fast that there has been no time in England for thinking about the education of railway managers. Much attention is given to this matter in Germany; and, unless the English railways are to continue to be administered by rule of thumb, without knowledge of their own conditions, much less of the conditions of the railways of other countries, some method of education will have to be devised by the English railway companies in their own interests. Institutes of bankers, of chartered accountants, etc., do a good deal for professional education; but there is absolutely no provision in England for anything of the kind in connection with railways.

As regards the general tenor of English railway policy, it may be said in general terms that the dozen great lines which may be regarded for practical purposes as the English railway system form together a *quasi*-public insti-

---

* As, for example, on the side of the railways, the objection to giving adequate statistics, on the ground that " it is better for the public not to know too much "; and, on the side of the traders, that the interests of individual classes of traders alone ought to be considered.

† *Cf.* diagram in *Atti della Commissione d' Inchiesta sull' Exercizio delle Ferrovie Italiane*, 1884, Parte II., vol. ii. p. 957.

tution, which might be put in the same category as the Bank of England. England could no more allow the London & North-western Railway Company to shut up its line and go into liquidation than it could allow the Bank of England to close its doors and go into the bankruptcy court. Both are creatures of statute, with strict limitation of the element of private initiative preserved to them by the nature of their charters. Neither can make any departure out of a well-beaten track without the sanction of Parliament. In the case of the railway companies it is not necessary to go back to the "musty charters of 1840" (although the statute of limitations does not apply to acts of Parliament); every important limitation has been repeated and emphasized in every general railway act from then till now.

We may be quite ready to admit the dangers of State control, the inconveniences of it, the expensiveness of it; but it is plain that, however the English railways have kicked and protested, they have been bound hand and foot by the statutes, and they have never been strong enough to resist Parliament, backed up, as it has been in its relations with the railways, by public opinion. Never free, the railways have, for good or evil, been more and more definitely tied to the State.

The next few years will reveal how far private enterprise will bear the strain of intimate control in detail by a State department.

www.ingramcontent.com/pod-product-compliance
Lightning Source LLC
Chambersburg PA
CBHW031804090426
42739CB00008B/1157